WHY DON'T TIGERS EAT BANANAS?

By Katherine Smith

Consultant: Nicola Davies

WHY DON'T TIGERS EAT BANANAS?

Copyright © *ticktock* Entertainment Ltd 2004
First published in Great Britain in 2004 by *ticktock* Media Ltd.,
Unit 2, Orchard Business Centre, North Farm Road, Tunbridge Wells, Kent, TN2 3XF
We would like to thank: Meme Ltd and Elizabeth Wiggans.
ISBN 1 86007 513 4 PB
ISBN 1 86007 517 7 HB
Printed in China
A CIP catalogue record for this book is available from the British Library.

CONTENTS

Any words appearing in the text in bold, **like this**, are explained in the Glossary.

Why don't tigers eat bananas?

Because tigers are carnivores, so only eat meat.

Carnivores have special teeth to help them eat meat. The long, dagger-like teeth at the front of a tiger's mouth are called **canines**. Tigers use them to grab hold of their **prey**, and to deliver the killing bite! Their sharp side teeth help to slice up the food.

Tigers have 30 teeth. Their canines can be up to 90 mm long!

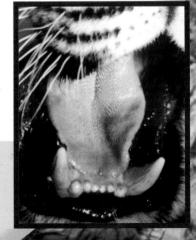

A tiger's tongue is rough. This helps it to lick all the meat off the skin and bones.

Tiger teeth can be gentle too. A mother uses them to carry her cubs around.

Tigers' sharp claws help them to seize hold of prey.

Why don't tigers have food bowls?

Because tigers live in the wild and hunt for their food!

When tigers hunt, they don't chase their prey. They are far too big and heavy to run far. Instead, tigers sneak up on their unsuspecting dinner, then POUNCE!

Tigers use their tails to help them balance when they run.

Tigers can run at speeds of up to 56 kilometres per hour, but only for a few seconds.

Tigers hunt small animals and birds, as well as deer, pigs, cattle, and antelope.

Tigers sometimes eat a whole antelope at one sitting, then don't eat again for days.

Why don't tigers have spots?

Because stripes help tigers hide when they hunt.

Tigers need to stay hidden when they hunt, so that they can surprise their prey. The black stripes on their orange fur help them to "disappear" when they are sneaking through the bushes and long grass. This is called **camouflage**.

A tiger has this special marking called the "wang mark" on its forehead.

Siberian tigers live in cold, snowy climates. They have much thicker fur than other tigers to keep them warm.

Tigers live in the jungles, swamps, forests, and grasslands of Asia.

No two tigers' stripes are exactly the same.

Some very **rare** tigers in India are completely white.

15

Why don't tigers live in groups?

Because adult tigers like to live and HUNT on their own.

Imagine how difficult it would be to sneak up on someone if you had lots of friends with you! It's just the same for tigers when they hunt. That's why you rarely see more than one tiger at once – unless it's a mother with her cubs.

Tigers leave **scent markings** and scratches on trees to mark their **territory**.

Tigers are an **endangered species**. There are only about 8,000 left in the world today.

The word for a group of tigers is a **streak**.

Why don't tigers need
torches to hunt
in the dark?

Because tigers have fantastic night **vision**!

Tigers use their senses of sight and hearing to hunt at night. Their eyes are specially adapted to see in the dark. In fact, they can see six times better than humans in dim light.

Most tigers have yellow eyes, but some rare, white tigers have blue eyes.

Tigers hunt mainly at night.

Tigers' eyes glow in the dark because they reflect light.

Tigers use their long whiskers to help them feel their way in the dark.

Why don't tiger cubs hatch from eggs?

Because tigers are **mammals** and, like nearly all *mammals*, they give birth to live **young**.

Tiger cubs are born blind, and weigh no more than a bag of sugar at birth. They feed on their mother's milk for the first few months of their lives. When they are big and strong enough, their mother teaches them to hunt.

If her cubs are in danger, a mother will carry them in her mouth to a safe place.

Cubs open their eyes when they are about two weeks old.

Tiger cubs feed on their mother's milk until they are six months old. Then, Mum teaches them how to hunt.

Tiger cubs leave their mother when they are about two to three years old.

There are usually two or three cubs in a **litter**, but often one dies.

Tiger PROFILE

Life span

15–25 years in the wild.

Size

2–3.5 metres in length, which means they can be as long as a big car!

Weight

227 kilograms or more, which is three times as much as a man!

Numbers

No one knows for sure how many tigers are left in the wild, but it is probably somewhere between 6,000 and 8,000.

Tigers
live in Asia.

Fact file

There are five different types of tiger:

Sumatran tigers

Bengal tigers

Siberian tigers (**Amur** tigers)

Indochinese tigers

South China tigers

Scientists believe tigers use their tails to communicate with other tigers.

Tigers can weigh as much as three grown men. The heaviest tiger ever recorded was a male Siberian tiger, weighing 465 kilograms. That's as much as six male human beings!

Tiger claws are 100 millimetres long, that's half the length of a pencil!

GLOSSARY

Camouflage — Colourings or markings on an animal or insect that allow it to blend in with its natural surroundings.

Canines — Strong pointed teeth.

Carnivores — Plants or animals that feed on the meat of other animals.

Endangered species — A species of animal that is in danger of being hunted by human beings or of losing its habitat (the place where it lives).

Litter — A group of young animals born to one mother at the same time.

Mammals	Animals that are warm-blooded and produce milk for their young.
Prey	An animal that is hunted for food by another animal.
Rare	An animal that is hard to find because there are so few left in the world.
Scent marking	A special smell left by an animal to show other animals that the territory is occupied.
Streak	The proper name for a group of tigers.
Territory	The area that one animal defends against other animals to keep its food supply and family safe.

INDEX